MW00698359

Book cover design by
Melissa Carlson Creative
www.MelissaCarlsonCreative.com

In Gratitude

I'd like to thank all my friends at the Transformational Leadership Council for their unending support and encouragement. Especially to those who contributed to this book in one way or another. A special thank you to my dear friends who gave of their talents to help me fulfill my dream to write this book, specifically;

Beth, Beverly, Brittany, Lori, Melissa, Nicole, Patty, and Bob.

Table of Contents

In Gratitude   3

Table of Contents   5

Foreword by Robert MacPhee: Hugs   7

Introduction   13

Proper Hugs   17

Hugs in Business   23

Hugging is Healthy   27

Angel Hugs   31

Mental Hugs   35

Hugs that Saved the Moment   39

Surprising Hugs   43

Manly Hugs   47

The Best Hug Ever   55

Be a Hugger   59

The Hug Movement   63

Epilogue   67

About the Author The Little SPARK   71

Edifications   73

Foreword by Robert MacPhee: Hugs

"Making the world a more loving place, one hug at a time..."
~Robert MacPhee

When I arrived in Santa Barbara in 1998 at Jack Canfield's "Breakthrough to Success" seminar, I had no idea what I was getting myself into. I was interested in being more successful in my business and I knew this meant improving me. But if you had told me what we were going to be doing to improve ourselves, I would have never gone.

This week-long seminar was life changing for me. It made me the person I am today. I learned a lot about myself, a lot about the world I live in, and a lot about the way I was connecting with the people around me.

On the very first day we were asked to stand up and do an exercise. It was an easy exercise, nothing scary, but the thought of doing it made me uncomfortable. The exercise was called "Hugs," and the instructions were simple, "mill around the room and get some hugs."

"Are you kidding me?" said the voice in my head. "Hugging a bunch of strangers? No way!" Every cell in my body wanted to turn and run out of the room. The presenter broke the ice with humorous instruction from the stage about how people hug incorrectly, for example, no bear hugs, burping the baby, A-frames, hit and runs or groping (see chapter 1). The bottom line was that I was being asked to hug a bunch of strangers. Really!?

I had grown up in a house where hugs were uncommon. It was the kind of house where if you had any questions about how babies were made there were books on the shelf you could read. I had loving parents, but expressing their love through physical contact was few and far between. So the idea of wandering around the room and hugging 300 plus total strangers was taking me way outside my comfort zone. If I could have made a run for it without humiliating myself, I might have, but clearly my best choice seemed to be to fake a smile, suck it up, and somehow get through it. Then maybe we would begin working on time management strategies.

Surprise! I made it through the first day alive. I also survived each of the six remaining days of the seminar where at least once each day we did the same exercise. In fact, by the end of the week, as we practiced, and as those strangers became friends sharing a powerful experience, the hugs became more and more comfortable. I ended up getting more hugs in a week than I would normally get in years. I felt a deep connection with all of those hugs. I felt the increased connection to people. **I realized that a warm, nurturing hug is simply put, a powerful way for two human beings to connect.**

At the end of the seminar I went home, back to my family, friends, and work. For a while, I shared more hugs with friends and family, but after a short period of time, I went back to my non-hugging ways. I was unwilling to ask for the hugs I wanted and unwilling to give the hugs I wanted to share unless I knew the other person wanted them. What happened to me was what happens to many people when they have a remarkable experience like the one I had at the seminar, the benefits failed to last.

I returned to the same event a year later because I had had such a fantastic experience the first time. Needless to say, on the first day when the "Hugs" exercise was announced, I was less surprised and uncomfortable. I was actually looking forward to it. I realized how I had been allowing myself to miss out on giving and receiving hugs if it made me uncomfortable. Because I felt like I was missing out on something valuable in giving and receiving hugs, I decided to do something about it.

I created a button with a simple logo on it that said, "ihug".

I began wearing it and sharing the buttons with others. It became a way to give and receive hugs I otherwise would have missed out on. People would ask me what the button meant. I would explain that it meant I like to give and receive hugs. Inevitably people would say, "me too," and we would share a hug. People began to ask me where they could get the buttons, so I printed up extras and set up a web page where people could buy them online, www.robertmacphee.com/ihug. It became a mini-movement! Imagine that, the guy who grew up receiving very few hugs was now "the hug guy."

Perhaps the greatest benefit of all of this visible conversation about hugging was within my own family. My children, who were very young when I attended the seminar, grew up in an environment where hugging and other healthy, nurturing physical touch was accepted and encouraged. Even my brothers, sister, and parents were drawn reluctantly into the hugging movement. Handshakes and high fives were replaced with warm, nurturing hugs.

Years later, my parents told me that if they had it to do all over again, one of the things they would change about their approach to parenting would to be more free and easy with physical touch, especially hugging.

Over the years I have learned the value of a simple hug. I'm thrilled LuAnn has created this book to share the "gospel" of hugging, and I hope reading it has the same impact for you that attending the seminar many years ago had on me – giving and receiving more hugs! Please avoid making this a temporary change. Somewhere out there is someone who needs a hug from you, and it would be a shame if they missed out on it because you, like me, were too uncomfortable to share. It's a movement! Are you with me?

Hug to Go... Join the movement!

Introduction

"Be a love pharmacist: dispense hugs like medicine-they are!"
~Terri Guillemets

A hug is a powerful tool connecting us to other human beings. I've always been an affectionate person, but I doubt that I have always used this tool in my life. I lived the majority of my life on autopilot in terms of personal touch and hugs. I never used hugs in a business setting; I saved hugs for family and friends and those who were open to hugging.

Several years ago, I discovered the book, the *Five Love Languages: The Secret to Love that Lasts,* by Gary D. Chapman. My husband and I took the quiz included with this book to learn how to communicate better with each other. The five love languages are words of affirmation, gift giving, acts of service (devotion), quality time, and physical touch. The test uncovers which of these languages gives you pleasure. My love language is personal touch. This is something I need in my life from others, so it was serendipitous that my first assignment at my first Transformational Leadership Council meeting was to bestow a hug upon each attendee as they arrived and departed over the course of the weekend.

The Transformational Leadership Council is an organization created by Jack Canfield, author of Chicken Soup for the Soul series and President of Canfield Success Principles. The organization is designed to bring transformational leaders together from around the world to support each other's visions and learn from one another. The first TLC meeting I attended was in Vail, Colorado, in 2008, and this is where my hug journey began.

Serving at the TLC events is an extraordinary blessing in my life, for which I am forever grateful to my friend, Dr. Ivan Misner, Founder & Chief Visionary Officer for Business Network International (BNI). He referred me to Guy Stickney, the TLC Meeting Director.

At that first meeting, Guy gave me the assignment to greet every one of the attendees with a hug upon their arrival and again when they departed. That's right; it was my "job" to hug everyone, to make each person feel welcomed and loved.

From the minute I arrived, before I knew the members, I was connected to them through the power of a hug. Hugs bring people together and create a connection of love and service. There is no judgment, no question, no doubt. Just love.

Then in 2011, Robert MacPhee, one of our speakers at the Passionate Life Summit, in San Diego, California gifted all of us with an "ihug" button. It was there I decided to wear the button as a way to warn people that I HUG. Soon it became a human experiment to see how people would react.

I remember my first experience while wearing the button. I was standing in the lobby waiting to direct people arriving for the conference. An older gentleman coming in for a Veterans

Reunion was standing in line at the front desk, and I caught him staring at me. He was reading the button. I could see the wheels turning in his head trying to figure out what it said. Then he blurted out "you hug?" I said "I do," and I proceeded to give him a big HUG.

Now, I give the buttons out to other people and ask them to report back to me with their stories. This is a basis for this book, to share my experiences and others while wearing the "ihug" button.

Hug to Go...Get your "ihug" button and send me your stories for the next book.

Proper Hugs

"We need 4 hugs a day for survival. We need 8 hugs a day
for maintenance. We need 12 hugs a day for growth."
- Virginia Satir, family therapist

Is there a proper way to hug? I hate to even suggest there is, as I would hate for people to avoid giving hugs in case they might do it wrong. Any hug, any human touch or connection is better than no hug at all. We. All. Need. Hugs.

Our world has created a sense of fear around touching other human beings. Teachers are told to keep their hands off the students because it may be misinterpreted as a sexual act rather than human comfort. In business, people fear it may be misinterpreted and lead to accusations of sexual harassment. So many people have stopped hugging.

Let's discuss some tips about proper hugging. A hug should feel comfortable and safe for both parties engaged in the embrace. Jack Canfield taught me this in one of his presentations and is similar to what Robert MacPhee referenced in the foreword of this book. The following are some tips I adapted from Jack on proper ways to hug:

1. People often hug right ear to right ear, when embracing. However, when we place our hearts together, by hugging left ear to left ear, we can share the love in our hearts during the embrace. This is my

hugging practice. I pour love from my heart into the other person as I am hugging them.

2. If you are hugging someone who is shorter than you, bend at the knees rather than sticking your backside into the air. The goal is to level the playing field; otherwise someone is going to have a sore back and the other a sore neck. I happen to be 4'11" tall, so this resonates with me. At one of the TLC meetings, when I first met Barnet Bain, Director, Milton's Secret, Author, *The Book of Doing and Being: Rediscovering Creativity in Life, Love and Work,* who is 6' 1" tall, he asked me to take a few steps up on the staircase before we embraced. It was awesome and so considerate of him to recognize the need for us to be at the same level for the hug to be comfortable and safe for both of us.

At other meetings, I have stood on the sidewalk curb or steps to deliver the hugs depending on the height of the person I was hugging to make it comfortable and safe for all involved.

Then there is Marc Pletzer, managing director of Fresh-academy GmpH, who is nearly 6'6" tall. Also a TLC member, when Marc and I hug it's best if he is sitting down so that we are then the same height. He has been known to get on his knees to give me a hug. That works too. Although less comfortable for him, I am sure.

3. Avoid burping the baby or patting someone on the back while in an embrace. My editor and I hugged good-bye after working on this section of the book, and she patted me on the back. It was funny to see the power of suggestion. Now she is conscious about how

she will hug people in the future. No burping the baby, please!

4. You may also want to avoid rubbing someone's back unless you know them very well. Rubbing the back is a more sensual experience. It also implies you are comforting them. When appropriate, this is a good thing.

5. Hugging while sitting down can be a challenge. In awkward situations, acknowledge it. For example, if you are sitting in the car trying to give someone a hello or goodbye hug, simply say, "I want to give you a hug." Both of you reaching in for the embrace can make the situation more comfortable.

6. Hugging people in a wheelchair is a similar situation. Ask permission to find out what makes them comfortable. I learned this from my friend Lori Colwill, who is in a wheelchair and loves receiving hugs as much as the next person. However, she wants to remind people that her wheelchair is an extension of her body. So never lean on someone's wheelchair or use it as an arm rest.

My brother Tom is in a wheelchair and loves getting hugs, too. He will ask people to give him a hug and let them know it is okay. Despite the awkwardness, you may feel, hugging someone in a wheelchair is similar to hugging someone shorter than you. Bend at the knees, go in for the hug left ear to left ear and allow the love energy to pour from your heart.

7. Hugs take time. Avoid the hug and run, similar to a quick peck on the cheek. Put love into every hug you give. I love this scene from The Big Bang Theory:

   Leonard: What was with the long hug?
   Penny: That was not a long hug.
   Leonard: It was at least five Mississippis, a standard hug is two Mississippis tops.

   If you recall the episode, you know Penny's hug was saying, "I'll miss you!"

Hugs can have many non-verbal meanings. The good news is, every one of those meanings has a positive impact on your emotional and physical being

"As a mode of communication, an embrace can express what can't be put into words. The embrace stimulates pleasurable feelings. It can be superficial, or very close and tight, but it is always charged with emotions." - Mabel Iam, author of The Love Diet.

Jack Canfield's version of Virginia Satir's quote at the beginning of this chapter is:

- four hugs a day for survival
- eight hugs a day for maintenance

- twelve hugs a day for growth
- sixteen hugs a day for transformation

In Mabel Iam's book, *The Love Diet*, she says the recommended hug daily allowance is:

- Four hugs are needed every day for basic sustenance.
- Eight hugs are necessary to stay in good shape.
- Twelve will help us grow as loving beings.
- Fifteen will help us strengthen our bodies' defense mechanisms.
- Twenty will guarantee happiness.
- Twenty-five hugs a day will vanquish any negative emotion.
- Thirty will make anybody glow.
- Forty will ensure success in everything you do.

"If you can perform 50hugs, you'll be very successful that day, but the most important thing is that you inspire happiness in each person that you hug because hugs are contagious that way." Mabel Iam

Hug to go...Get as many hugs as you can every day, in a comfortable and safe way!

Hugs in Business

"I need a hug job."
~Tony Delgrosso

How do you choose between a handshake and a hug? There's no right answer, except to be authentic. If you'll recall I adopted the "ihug" button from Robert McPhee as a way to caution people that I HUG. I wore this button in the business environment to warn people that I hug, and most often I still received the hug. Yet, I rarely assume people are open to it.

One year, the TLC decided to meet with the World Business Academy to talk about transformation in business with Fortune 500 and Fortune 100 company leaders. My assignment again was to hug each person upon arrival and departure. In my mind, I questioned how those CEOs would react to my hug. I wore my "ihug" button as a cautionary sign and proceeded with my assignment. **They all loved it!** Each and every one of the CEOs commented about how nice it was to receive a hug.

One CEO said to me, "WOW! Do you really give people hugs all the time?"

"Yeah, we do, it's our culture. We aim to make everyone feel loved and supported," I said.

Each day, they began to look forward to those hugs. Then they expected and loved it again when we gave them a good-bye hug.

I contacted Dr. Ivan Misner, Founder and Chief Visionary Officer of BNI (Business Network International) because I felt people looked at him as a non-hugger as an "all" business man. I wanted to get his perspective on the world of hugging. Ivan referred to himself as a "selective hugger" rather than a non-hugger. "Context is key," he said. "It depends on the environment or situation one is in, to get a sense of what's appropriate. I do believe there has been a shift in the world in the last five years. Twenty years ago, I almost never saw hugging in business." Now in the right context it can be acceptable. As with BNI, it is about building relationships. "I never hug a stranger. Over time, when relationships have grown to a certain level then hugging becomes more acceptable - with people I know, like and trust."

For example, in a TLC meeting or self-development conference, one might expect to get hugs. He commented on my story that the CEOs who came to the TLC for a business meeting, were probably more open to my hugs than if they had arrived at a meeting with bankers and had been greeted by hugs. Because they knew the context was about transformation.

I shared with Ivan, my story of being approached by a BNI Leadership Team member, who was complaining about a fellow Director Consultant. She was offending people by forcing them to hug her all the time. I said, "You better talk to someone other than me because I am a hugger." She said, "LuAnn if I ask you to stop you will. This other person is insisting that people hug her and it is making people uncomfortable."

Ivan was surprised to find out that a woman was complaining about another woman hugging her. He reflected that he has heard many a time when women complained about men hugging them, but never a woman hugging another woman. Here again it is about context and honoring other people's boundaries. People may have had a negative experience, even a sexual attack, which has made them uncomfortable with other people touching them. We must be sensitive to this.

Ivan's recommendation was to ask people if it's okay to give them a hug. He says people often ask him and are pleasantly surprised that he is open to it. "I have been conditioned by the TLC," he said. "So, I hug much more often and even surprise some of the people I have known for years, when I greet them with a hug."

"After I was given the award by the TLC of being a Tree Hugger...well if I can hug a tree, I can surely hug people." Ivan said.

When I travel on business, I have a tendency to get my rest by sleeping on the plane. On one trip, I slept the whole flight. I was in the back of the plane, so I decided to wait for all the other passengers to get off before I disembarked. I had forgotten I was wearing my "ihug" button. As I walked down the aisle, the flight attendant looked at me and with a pouty voice said, "I hug too." I asked, "Do you need a hug?" She responded, "Yes, I do!" So of course, you know what happened.

It's interesting how seriously we take our businesses. People could take a lesson from Southwest Airlines and have a little more fun with the culture of their organizations. Did you know the 35,000 employees of Southwest Airlines have replaced handshakes with hugging and even kissing? To learn more about the culture of their organization, read the book, *Nuts, Southwest Airlines' Crazy Recipe for Business and Personal Success*, by Kevin Freiberg. Even the title is fun!

Another fabulous hug story happened during a business luncheon. I was wearing my "ihug" button of course, and the waitress exclaimed, "Oh, I love your button." So I stood and gave her a hug. Because she was so excited about it, I gave her the button. She put it on immediately. The next time I was in the restaurant she said, "There's my favorite hug lady." We shared another hug. I asked where her "ihug" button was. She said, "My manager won't let me wear it because it isn't part of the uniform standards."

Well maybe it should be. Think of the powerful statement you could make to the world if you incorporated hugs as a part of your customer service standards. Anybody brave enough to try? Please write to me and tell me about it.

Hug to Go...The business environment has become so stark and cold it's no wonder people are full of stress and anxiety. We need human touch – we need HUGS! Give them appropriately.

Hugging is Healthy

"Everybody needs a hug. It changes your metabolism."
~Leo Buscaglia

According to *The Hug Therapy* book, by Kathleen Keating, "Hugging is healthy. It helps the body's immune system, it keeps you healthier, it cures depression, it reduces stress, it induces sleep, it's invigorating, it's rejuvenating, it has no unpleasant side effects, and hugging is nothing less than a miracle drug.

Hugging is all natural. It is organic, naturally sweet, no pesticides, no preservatives, no artificial ingredients and 100 percent wholesome.

Hugging is practically perfect. There are no movable parts, no batteries to wear out, no periodic check-ups, low energy consumption, high energy yield, inflation proof, nonfattening, no monthly payments, no insurance requirements, theft-proof, nontaxable, nonpolluting and, of course, fully returnable."

There is even Scientific Evidence that a Hug-a-Day Can Save Your Life:

"Scientists are increasingly interested in the possibility that positive emotions can be good for your health. This study has reinforced research findings that support from a partner, in this case, a hug from a loved one can have beneficial effects on heart health."

Dr. Manny Alvarez/AH (Feb. 5th, 2007)

The act of hugging is life itself, according to Mabel Iams, author of The Life Diet in her chapter called The Hug Diet:

This diet is terrific because the act of hugging transfers energy and causes positive emotional stimulation, resulting in happiness. Physical contact and stimulation are absolutely necessary for our overall well-being.

The arms wrapped around the neck or waist, with the faces touching cheek-to-cheek is, no doubt, the most commonly practiced hug as a demonstration of affection.

The cultural differences of how hugging is practiced around the world are fascinating to observe. An embrace is intimately connected with friendship and deep affection. An embrace expresses special feelings when it is offered with care, respect, and love. Even those who are shy can express how they truly feel, and even cure themselves of shyness in the process.

Effects and benefits of the hug diet:

- Can be used to offer an enthusiastic greeting.
- Helps overcome fear and worry.
- Awakens the senses.
- Strengthens self-esteem.
- Aids in reconciliation attempts.
- Dissipates tension and nervousness.

- Affirms the other person thus helping us open to love.
- Fills the empty spaces in our lives.
- The hug lifts us out of a time of monotony or stress.
- Puts an end to depression.
- Increases one's desire to live.
- Cures shyness.
- Acts as a sexual stimulant.
- Heightens sex-appeal.
- Helps us to feel loved and appreciated.
- A sexually-charged hug helps a couple feel even more united.

Many scientific and psychological studies have shown that for premature babies who have not had sufficient physical contact, a small hug can help them to grow and get stronger. Physical contact has a positive effect on children's development, emotionally, and intellectually.

Hugs cause detectable physiological changes in people who give the hug or receive it. For the elderly, hugs help them ward off feelings of isolation. Because of emotional ups and downs we all experience after a certain age we all need to get our recommended daily allowance of hugs.

Hug to Go...Create your own human experiment and count how many hugs you give in a day. See if you can get up to 50 or more for the benefit of your health.

Angel Hugs

"A hug connects heaven and earth."
~Martin Rutte, Founder of ProjectHeavenonEarth.com

One of my greatest lessons about hugs came at a TLC meeting I attended in Maui, in January 2015. Doreen Virtue talked about Angels speaking to us. She said they speak to us in all kinds of ways. For example, it may be the voice of another human being versus a mystical voice coming out of nowhere. I loved Doreen's presentation and found myself enthralled in her message. Was she speaking to me, or was it the angels coming through her that were actually speaking to me?

The morning after this presentation I was meditating in the shower, and I burst out laughing. The Angels were speaking to me in the voices in my head and here is what they said...

"LuAnn, you silly woman, the messages you hear when people whisper in your ear during a HUG are the voices of your Angels. Every time someone whispers in your ear, it's the Angels speaking to you, telling you how wonderful you are." What a blessing! Think about it. How would it shift your world, if you really took to heart everything anyone ever whispered in your ear during a hug or otherwise.

With every hug, I started listening more intently to the messages coming through other people. Here are some of the messages that resonated with me while embracing others...

"You are amazing. You know that right? Really, you know that, right!" said Dr. Sue Morter, Master of Bio-Energetic Medicine and Quantum Field visionary.

"You are f****** outrageous. No really I mean it. You are amazing. I hope you know that," said Rick Foster, President of Foster, Hicks & Associates.

"You're the best hugger," said Lisa Garr, Creator of the Aware Show

"You are a voracious hugger," said Hari Lubin, father of Karin Lubin, General Manager of the Passion Test programs.

"I am attracted to something in your heart," said Hana Honda, daughter of Ken Honda, bestselling author of more than 60 self-development books in Japan.

"You are the world's best hugger," said GP Walsh, Creator of INNER RECONCILIATION, Spiritual Teacher, Speaker, Author, Storyteller, and Master Coach

During the departing hug I received from Dr. Sue Morter, she said to me, "Congratulations, you are birthing something. It is so beautiful to watch. I don't know what it is, but a shift is coming." It was at this meeting the idea for the "ihug" book was birthed, and I started to formulate a plan. (Although it has been a lot longer gestation period than a normal pregnancy.)

Hug to Go...You have messages like this coming to you too. Listen to your Angels and give birth to it.

Mental Hugs

"Sometimes a silent hug is the only thing to say."
~Robert Brault

This to me is a fascinating chapter because it is about something even more than the physical touch. I have told you "personal touch" feeds my soul. But for other people, personal touch is unacceptable. We huggers can be seen as invading their space, so there is the mental hug. Read this excerpt from the *NY Times* bestseller *Love for No Reason,* by Marci Shimoff with Carol Kline.

Co-author, Carol Kline, did the following fun experiment with "mental hugs" to ramp up her loving attention:

My morning bike ride always takes me past a stream of walkers, runners, and other bicyclists. I'm a naturally friendly person, and I like to smile and say good morning to everyone I pass. But sometimes I feel quiet or don't want to interrupt someone else's reverie, so I also make a point to "beam love" at the people I meet, whether I greet them physically or not. Some people smile back and others don't respond at all. (Though it's interesting that 99% of the dogs I encounter seem to be able to feel my love beam. They always turn to look at me with interest.)

One day, after having just read the research about the health benefits of hugging, I decided to turn it up a notch. Instead of just beaming love, I gave each person I passed a "mental hug."

I imagined taking each person, old, young, man or woman, in my arms and giving them a warm, sincere embrace. The experience was amazing. I could feel the energy in my body become stronger, brighter, and more loving each time I did it.

The heart-opening power of mental hugs is based on two simple facts:

1. *The act of hugging is good for you.* Studies show that if you hug someone for six seconds or more, your body produces mood-lifting chemicals that promote bonding with others, like oxytocin and serotonin. Hugging also lowers your blood pressure, gives your immune system a boost, and can diminish your experience of physical pain.

2. *Visualizing a physical action can give you many of the same benefits as the real thing.* When we *imagine* doing something, the same centers in the brain are activated as when we physically *do* the action. In imagined hugs, the reward centers are busy distributing feel-good chemistry to your cells, and the insula—a part of the brain that relates to embodied experience—is also activated. You can enjoy the same juicy feeling in your cells you would get from hugging the person.

And based on the Institute of HeartMath research about the power of the heart's electromagnetic field, we know that sending mental hugs is good for the huggee too—they're walking (or bicycling) right through your positively charged heart field. When you give mental hugs, love does the happy dance! So you can understand why Carol is as high as a kite by the time she finishes her morning rides.

Here is another story from my good friend, Ruth Tongen, on her experience wearing the "ihug" button. I met Ruth when she attended a Woman in Spirituality Workshop, in Mankato, where I was presenting. Perhaps, this is an instance where a mental hug could have been given to shift the other person's mood:

I got to the airport, went through the pre-check line and got pulled aside for the random screening. (This happened going both directions.)

I stepped into the booth to be scanned. They then said I'd need to be patted down. A TSA agent, who was obviously having a bad day, or life, came over to pat me down. I instinctively raised my arms like you do in the scanning booth. She yelled out, "Put your arms down!" and under her breath said, "Zheezh". She patted me down and then looked at the screen and saw that it was my "ihug" button I was wearing that had set it off. She asked me why on earth I thought I could go through the system wearing that and dressed me down.

I had lots of comeback lines in my head, but bit my tongue. I chuckled afterward thinking she needed a hug, but I doubt she was open for one. And after she was finished, I needed a hug. I made a point to hug a lot when I got home.

You can be sure I will still be wearing my button often to get all the hugs I need!

Hug to Go...If physical touch is uncomfortable, practice giving mental hugs. Everyone benefits!

Hugs that Saved the Moment

"If you're angry at a loved one, hug that person. And mean it. You may not want to hug-which is all the more reason to do so. It's hard to stay angry when someone shows they love you, and that's precisely what happens when we hug each other."
~Walter Anderson, The Confidence Course

My obsession with the impact of Hugs intensified at our Get Connected 2012 Conference in Miami. This was a networking conference my business partner and I held to help business professionals sharpen their networking skills. The key is that I had a business partner and we were hosting a conference together with many of our BNI colleagues in the audience. I made a huge, embarrassing mistake that caused a great deal of tension between my business partner and me. No one else knew what happened, and there is really no need to dig up old skeletons. Think about your worst transgression in front of one of your peers and you'll feel my pain. Although only she and I knew exactly what happened, I am sure everyone could sense the tension.

Well, at least one person could tell for sure, our emcee, Tony Wolfe, Voice Actor. Tony knew nothing of what had transpired, but he came to me and asked if I was okay? "Is there anything I can do," he said. There was no fixing it; only a comforting hug helped ease the pain. Afterward, without a word spoken, Tony hugged me every time he saw me. He hugged me when I was standing in the back of the room and while we passed each other in the hall. I received more hugs that weekend than any other event in my life. And I needed every one of those hugs to cut through the tension so I could persevere through the event.

At the end of the event, I was at the airport headed for my flight. I was on one of those moving walk ways and spotted Tony sitting at his gate. I yelled out his name and he came running alongside the walkway to give me a good-bye hug. Funny, we rushed together with two open arms like two airplanes coming in to hug each other, like when you were children rushing each other with open arms. I laughed; it was an airplane hug, at the airport.

The point is, a hug can shift and change any situation. It can also create lifelong friendships when you share a human connection like no other.

Brian Hillard is the spouse of one of our TLC Members, and ever since I met him we have had a special hug connection. I asked Brian to share with us his experience with hugs in his work with the homeless.

Having worked with the homeless for over 40 years, Brian has had the privilege of actually witnessing the transformational power of a loving hug with good people living in extremely harsh conditions each and every day. On the streets hugs aren't dispersed freely or frequently. In fact, they are often earned with patience and a display of kindness that originates from an open heart and a willingness to listen to their life stories without judgment—only unconditional love.

If you are fortunate enough to be invited into their orbit for a hug, the first few can provide comfort, warmth, and might generate a smile or a moment of joy. As the hugs continue, you can actually feel their stress and anxieties wash away as they begin to feel acknowledged. Some, even for a precious moment, feel loved and experience a renewed sense of dignity. Over time something magical can happen. Grace sometimes envelops our loving exchanges and the hugs feel as though they are becoming a sacred expression between two souls devoted to a higher form of friendship.

Then, something special takes hold—trust takes root and the relationship begins to blossom. As healing begins, the conversations become more intimate, vulnerable, and honest. Your new friend might find the courage to ask for medical help or assistance with an addiction. This may lead to a roof over their head which is their best outcome. And it all started from a caring embrace, a powerful heart to heart hug.

Hug to Go…Bless someone with a hug in their hour of need.

Surprising Hugs

"A hug is like a boomerang—you get it back right away."
~Bil Keane, "Family Circus"

Surprising, or is it a universal attraction? Depending on your level of conscious awareness, you may call it surprising. I, however, look at things that appear to be surprising, or out of the blue, as universal intervention in my life. Here's an example of universal intervention that began with a hug.

I attended a conference in Cancun, Mexico, on the Energy Codes with Dr. Sue Morter. If you ever have the opportunity to attend this program, I highly recommend it. The teachings of this conference get you in touch with your true essence, the energy that is you. We all know we are made of energy, but to get in touch with the vibrations is another whole level of being. I was floating at the end of the event. It was in a place of bliss, a place I wanted to stay forever.

The tides turned when I arrived at the airport. My flight home was canceled, and I instantly felt alone and afraid. All the conference attendees had gone their separate ways and I was the only one left in Mexico. My feelings overwhelmed me. My mind and emotions went down the rabbit hole. I panicked! Where will I stay? How will I afford it? How will I get there? Will I be out on the streets?

The airline was less than helpful. There was a language barrier and I was uncertain what was going to happen next.

Instructions were disjointed at best. Stand in this line. Go get your luggage. Get in this line to retrieve your paperwork. Stand in that line to get re-ticketed. Once I met the ticket agent, he informed me the new flights would be in two days, and all hotels are sold out. The ticket agent then pointed to a young man in a pink shirt and said, "He is trying to help people, check with him." Tears streamed down my cheeks, and I could no longer maintain composure."

The young man in the pink shirt turned out to be helpful. He arranged transportation to the hotel, and a two-night stay with meals included. He was pointing me in the direction of my transportation when a gentleman walked up to me and said, "Tough day huh? You look like you could use a hug."

I said, "I do." And we embraced in a big hug. As we released our embrace, I reached for my pin located on the collar of my jacket and said, "Thank you, I needed that." But there was no button there. My energy attracted him and his embrace.

Almost in the same instant as we released from our hug, he motioned to his left and said, "I never give people hugs, this is my wife, ask her." He was an angel sent from above to let me know that everything was going to be okay. My mood shifted, and I was lighter and more peaceful.

I was whisked off to my hotel, feeling confident that I was safe. I then ran into the same gentleman again on the hotel elevator and several more times at the hotel. It always seemed to be in a fleeting moment, on or off the elevator when there was little time to stop and chat. However, the afternoon of the second day, we bumped into each other at the poolside bar. I took this opportunity to thank him again and learn more about him and his family.

All I remember now is that his name was Sam, and he was a coal miner from Colorado. More importantly, I remember how he made me feel. How he swooped in like an angel and shifted my entire mood. The two days stuck in Cancun were peaceful, and I was able to reflect on the extreme emotional shift. I had gone from floating on my energy being to hibernating in my protective self and then back to peace. While writing this, it is a good reminder that we have the ability to make that shift when we can consciously recognize our behavior. A simple hug will always help me make that shift.

So, if you see someone in distress, give them a HUG!

Hug to Go...A hug given is a hug received.

Manly Hugs

"There's something in a simple hug
that always warms the heart,
it welcomes us back home
and makes it easier to part."
~ Johnny Ray Ryder, Jr., "A simple hug."

"Men are not notoriously huggers. In fact, men are not notorious for allowing themselves to express much emotion at all." This was shared with me by my new friend, Z. Newell, Author & Inspirational Speaker (he goes by Z). When I met Z, I gave him a big hug as is standard operating procedure for me. He noticed my "ihug" button and exclaimed. "I have a story for you", so here is Z's story.

About 15 years ago, I stumbled across an unusual group of men in a non-profit organization called The Mankind Project. I can't go into detail about the processes we use in our New Warrior Training Adventures, but suffice it to say, in our own loving and magical way, we go about the task of helping men realize they have feelings and emotions at their fingertips. A man is permitted to feel anger, sadness, shame, joy and yes, fear, and are allowed to be authentic and vulnerable.

Anger is one of the only feelings that adolescent boys seem to have explicit permission to express. The notion that "Boys don't cry!" is all too common. Crying is equated with being weak or perhaps even a "sissy". So on this weekend, when New Warrior Training Adventure begins, men have a chance to safely explore many of those buried feelings. You might even say they "wake up" and begin to realize there is a whole new way they can show up in the world. A "new warrior" way of being, where, for example, anger may still exist, but it is used to protect and defend rather than inflict damage on others.

So what, you may ask, does any of this have to do with hugs?

Once our adventuresome men experience this men's training, it is safe to say that they are now ready to go much deeper within themselves not only to feel those emotions but to take responsibility for their actions and become men with a higher level of ownership and integrity in their lives. This might express itself as deep conversation and exchanges unlike those of the typical man hanging around talking about sports and women. I have had many such deep conversations with other men over the years.

During this weekend, a few other outward behavioral shifts take place. One is that men seem to smile more and be lighthearted. The burden of carrying all of that anger and stuffed feelings is somehow lifted. A second change is a customary language slang that we tend to use within this organization. When a man says something that is profoundly true for him, it might well be the case that it is true for another man listening as well. To that end, in meetings and exchanges a man might raise his hand to say "that's true for me too," or he might say "Aho!" meaning simply I hear you brother and that resonates with me.

The third significantly different behavioral shift is that men "hug" each other. Yes, no more shaking hands, they embrace openly. It's a beautiful thing to be hugging another human being that's not just a family member at a holiday gathering.

So, what is my point? Well, it's a simple, there's no other way for me to describe the profound shift in men that happens without really experiencing it for yourself. The following story is an example of the powerful effects of men's personal transformation at work.

Imagine this...

Every morning you stop at the same coffee shop. You're sitting there quietly catching up on some projects. Because you're always at the same coffee shop, you begin to notice the same people who also frequent that coffee shop.

At some point, you begin to observe some of the same people coming and going, and you feel you practically know them, even if you've never spoken to them before. You've been watching one particular group of men who are all construction workers or contractors and have the habit of stopping in to that coffee shop on their way to work each morning. In fact, they usually sit close enough for you to overhear their conversations. You even know some of them by name by now. There seems to be a part of you that is generally entertained listening to these guys jabbering about every-day stuff while you sit across the room pecking away on your laptop trying to solve the bigger, perhaps more important problems in the world. After all, they are just lowly laborers.

Given the nature of their work, those conversations pretty typically go something like this...

The first two guys, Joe and Harry, get their coffee from the counter and sit down at the table.

Joe: "What you got goin' on today?"

Harry: "Oh, I've got to put a toilet in."

Just then Sam walks in, grabs his coffee and sits down with them.

Sam: "Someone stole my Skilsaw yesterday," he tells them.

"Damn!" they both reply in unison.

Finally, the fourth man, Skip, walks up to the table with his coffee and sits down.

Skip says, "My back is aching like crazy again today! I've really got to find me another line of work sometime soon."

Then Joe and Harry get up from the table and announce that they've got to go to work.

Sam and Skip stay seated and tell them to have a good day. "See you guys here tomorrow morning."

And there you have it...the profound exchange of a few men BEFORE their major transformational men's weekend experience.

This brings us full circle to experiencing the power of hugging which is, in fact, the subject we are addressing here.

There is no way for me to express this better than to share with you the scene at that same coffee shop a couple of weeks later after these men have all gone through their powerful mankind weekend experience...

Once again you find yourself sitting at your laptop sipping your latte, and waiting for the other folks to come streaming through the doors for their daily coffee. Admit it; you're self-employed, so you love working at the coffee shop because of the distractions.

So here they come, like clockwork. You over hear them talking about going to some kind of a men's thing over the weekend, but you doubt that much will probably ever shift in these common folk, as that quiet little voice in your head continues to judge them.

And now, the post-weekend newly transformed men enter the scene once again...

You spot the first two guys, Joe and Harry, as they approach each other outside the coffee shop door. They are both smiling as they approach each other and embrace with a beautiful hug.

You are shocked as you peer through the window. It seems very out of character for the two men. "Maybe someone died and they're just consoling each other," you think to yourself.

The two of them get their coffee as usual and then sit down at the table next to you.

Joe: "What you got goin' on today?"

Harry: "Oh, I've got to put another toilet in."

Joe: "Aho!"

Just then Sam walks in, grabs his coffee and approaches them. Joe and Harry stand up from the table and each embrace Sam with a beautiful hug. Then they all sit down and resume their visit.

Sam: "I bought a new Skill Saw to replace the one that got stolen," says Sam.

Suddenly Joe and Harry respond simultaneously with a robust, "Aho!"

Just then, the fourth regular arrives. Skip walks up to the table with his coffee in hand.

Joe, Harry, and Skip all jump to their feet and one at a time embrace Skip with a beautiful, genuine hug.

Then they all sit down and the conversation resumes...

Skip says, "My back is aching like crazy AGAIN today! I've really got to find me another line of work sometime soon."

Joe, Harry, and Skip: "AHO!"

Then Joe and Harry get up from the table and announce that they've got to get to work.

Sam and Skip get up immediately, and you sit there with your jaw open observing a series of ensuing hugs, as each of the two men leaving receives their departing hug from Sam and Skip.

Sam and Skip sit back down.

Sam says, "Have a good day. See you guys here tomorrow morning at the usual time."

Joe and Harry: "AHO!"...and off they go, both with joyful smiles across their faces.

You can't say for sure what just happened, but somehow you sense that these are not the same man that you have seen in this very coffee shop over and over again for the better part of the past few months.

Something inside of you suddenly shifts although you can't quite put your finger on it. You wish you knew what was different about their relationship.

And then suddenly, unlike the introverted self that you know yourself to be, you turn to the two remaining men seated at the table next to you and say, "Hey, I couldn't help but overhear you guys talking about this men's weekend thing a couple of weeks ago. You seem just a little bit different now."

Sam and Skip look at each other with a twinkle in their eye, and both break into huge, joyous smiles.

"Hey brother... Why don't you pull up a chair and bring your coffee over here and join us?"

And their conversation and friendship begins...

Hug to Go... Men need Hugs Too

The Best Hug Ever

"Millions and millions of years would still not give me half enough time to describe that tiny instant of all eternity when you put your arms around me and I put my arms around you."
~Jacques Prevert

I was sitting by my fireplace one December evening, reading the *Four Agreements* by don Miguel Ruiz. I had been introduced to the book by a colleague, someone other than my TLC friends, interestingly enough. While deeply engrossed in this fascinating book I received a phone call from none other than, don Miguel himself. Talk about divine intervention. I nearly fell off my chair.

He called because he had been invited to join the TLC, and he was seeking my assistance to register. I was awe struck and honored to speak to him. I could hardly wait to meet him in person. I am always amazed at the blessings I receive from my connection to this organization.

In January, when don Miguel arrived at the TLC, I gave him a hug. It was different than any other hug I had ever received. Perhaps it's because we are the same height and our hearts connected immediately. But I believe it's because he exudes "unconditional love" like no other person I have ever met. I melted in his arms and wanted the embrace to last forever. The spiritual purity that comes from him is intoxicating. We all have this gift if we open our hearts with each and every hug we give. Hold on, feel it, pour out the love in your heart, in your entire being every time you reach out to give someone a hug.

Unconditional love means I love you no matter what happens. It is a feeling, a spirit connection, the source of all that is. It is I love you despite the circumstances. Whereas, conditional love is based on certain conditions, for example, "I love you because you are beautiful or smart or funny." You are putting conditions on love and stating you will only love that person as long as they are beautiful, smart, or funny.

After reading don Miguel's book, I challenged myself to live by the four agreements he shared in his book. However, I asked don Miguel if I could revise them to remove the k'not'ty words. I have provided my examples below.

The Four Agreements are:

1. **Be Impeccable with your Word:** Speak with integrity. Say only what you mean. Avoid using the Word to speak against yourself or to gossip about others. Use the power of your Word in the direction of truth and love.

2. **Don't Take Anything Personally (Take Nothing Personally)**
   Nothing others do is because of you. What others say and do is a projection of their own reality, their own dream. When you are immune to the opinions and

actions of others, you won't be the victim of needless suffering.

3. Don't Make Assumptions (Make No Assumptions)

Find the courage to ask questions and to express what you really want. Communicate with others as clearly as you can to avoid misunderstandings, sadness, and drama. With just this one agreement, you can completely transform your life.

4. Always Do Your Best

Your best is going to change from moment to moment; it will be different when you are healthy as opposed to sick. Under any circumstance, simply do your best and you will avoid self-judgment, self-abuse, and regret.

With don Miguel's permission I changed Don't Take Anything Personally to Take Nothing Personally and Don't Make Assumptions to Make No Assumptions, in my personal copy of his book. Because...

According to Bob Nicoll, author of Remember the Ice, negative words are referred to as "k-notty" words, because they turn your message into knots. Those words include not, and the hit list six...not, don't, won't, can't, wouldn't, couldn't, shouldn't, and the almighty should that only places blame on you or me depending on how it's used in a sentence. So, stop "shoulding" all over yourself.

Eliminating these words from your language also speaks to the concept of "being impeccable with your words." They are all negative and evoke contraction in the body. Imagine that, they are called contractions in the English language. Get it?

Remember the chapter on Angel voices speaking to me during hugs; we can all be those voices in other people's ears by being impeccable with our words as we exude love from our heart with every embrace (and eliminate the knotty words).

Hug to Go...Exude love from your heart in every hug!

Be a Hugger

"You are a voracious hugger."
~Hari Lubin

One of my mentors is Janet Bray Attwood, co-author of the New York Times bestseller, The Passion Test. I am also a Passion Test Facilitator, and for many years planned and participated in many Passion Test events. At these events, we create what we call the "Love Bubble," which is a swirling vortex of loving energy that begins and ends with hugs.

Similar to the TLC meetings, every person who attends our events receives a hug when they arrive and depart, and every chance in between. It is the way we start and conclude our day. The more hugs, the better. In doing so, we infuse the space around us with positive energy, love, and divine human connection.

I remember at one meeting in San Diego; I was being particularly vigilant in hugging everyone, at every possible moment. I believe it was the meeting when Robert McPhee first spoke to the team of facilitators, and when I received my first "ihug" button. I was hooked. I wore it every day. Thus the experiment began.

One of our participants, Hari Lubin (God rest his soul), was there with his daughter Karin Lubin, who is the General Manager of The Passion Test Programs. Karin was managing the event, and I was one of the volunteers in charge of registration. I was stationed in the lobby hugging people. Karin said to me, "My dad loves you and all your hugs." I made a conscious effort to hug Hari every time he passed by me, just as Tony Wolfe had done for me. Later, Hari came up to me and called me a voracious hugger.

The following year we created t-shirts for all of our volunteers with the title, "Master Hugger" on the back. On the front of the t-shirt, we included the unique contribution statement of our organization, "Inspiring Transformation Through Love." Our organization truly inspires transformation through love, and our hugging practice is just one of the tools we use to create the "Love Bubble" at every event.

Most recently, I was assisting at a course as a Master Trainer for the Passion Test for Business facilitators. I was playing dual roles. In the morning as everyone arrived for the day, I was at the door to make sure each and every person received a good morning hug. Many of them knew I was working on this book, and they loved being a part of the story as much as the hug itself. It never fails, everyone says to me, "You are a great hugger" or "You give great hugs!"

This day was no exception. I was due to present the first topic. When called to the stage, I ran up to the front of the room with a bold and boisterous "Gooooood Morning PTB." I was so excited to be living my passion, speaking and training people in a message I love. More importantly, I was excited about what had just happened to me. It was another case of universal intervention.

You see, I had decided in that moment to share with them Jack Canfield's quote about the number of hugs you need a day for transformation. Because Jack's quote noted earlier in this book says 16 hugs a day create transformation. I had just hugged 16 participants as they arrived that morning, therefore creating my own transformation for the day.

I Googled Jack's quote on my phone and what came up? An article I had written for the Rochester Women's Magazine on hugs. Because of course, I had used that quote in the article. How amazing though, that in all the times Jack Canfield has probably used that quote. On that particular day, it was my article that came up #1 on Google. Thus a universal intervention once again, as I created the "Love Bubble" in that room.

Hug to Go...Be a hugger! Create the Love Bubble in the world. We need it!

The Hug Movement

"I love hugging. I wish I was an octopus, so I could hug ten people at a time."
~Drew Barrymore

My intention with this book was to share some joyful stories with others about my journey with hugs. What I have experienced and what I have learned. I hope I have brought you some joy and laughter.

As my friend, Robert MacPhee said in the foreword, hugs have become a movement, and it is one that I want to be a part of spreading in this world. Now more than ever we need the powerful human connection of hugs.

You see I am simply a joy giver. I want people to feel the joy of living. Hugs bring that in an instant. The more instances you have with a hug in joy. The more fulfilled your life will feel.

There is no original idea and this is no different. It is simply my attempt to remind people of the value of a hug and what a powerful human connection it is.

I have quoted many other people in the book, shared their research and their stories. In addition, there are many other activities happening in our world around hugs. National Hugging Day was established in the United States in 1986 as January 21st. The Free Hugs campaign in its present form was started by Joan Mann in June of 2004. There is the FREE Hugs Project, where the gentleman was captured on video hugging police officers in Charlotte and Dallas after riots. And a woman from Chicago who has a Facebook campaign to create Global Free Hug Day on the first Saturday of May, where she is promoting that people take up post on a public street in their city and give out free hugs.

However you get involved, do it in a meaningful way for yourself and the people around you. Whether you're hugging the masses, getting your 50 hugs a day, or just one hug to a person in need. Just open your arms, your hearts, and your minds to embrace others.

With that said, I'd like to share one more personal story about Bill. I met Bill shortly after his wife passed away. Bill is retired, lives alone now, and has limited contact with his children. Bill stops in the local Bar & Grill just to be with people. When I met Bill over a year & half ago, I was, of course, wearing my "ihug" button. He commented, "I like your button." He shared with me how lonely he is and how much he longs for the human touch of a simply hug. I am sure the rest of the story is obvious. Bill and I embraced then, and we do every time I see him at our favorite local established. I feel blessed to share these moments with Bill and uplift his spirits just a little bit with each of those warm embraces.

On the day I was writing this chapter of the book, I opened a book of devotions that my dear friend Patty Blakesley gave me named, **hugs: Daily Inspirations for Women** (Copy @ 2006 by Howard Books) to this message...

Opportunities to Encourage

Barnabas (an early follower of Jesus whose name meant "Son of Encouragement") was known for his kindness and for his ability to encourage others. Today, as citizens of a difficult world, we must seek to imitate the "Son of Encouragement".

We imitate Barnabas when we offer hugs and kind words to loved ones. We imitate Barnabas when our actions give credence to our beliefs. We imitate Barnabas when we are generous with our possessions and with our praise. We imitate Barnabas when we give hope to the hopeless and encouragement to the downtrodden.

Today we, like Barnabas, can literally change the world one person – and one hug – at a time. And that is precisely what we should do.

Hug to Go...Make the world a more loving place, one hug at a time. Get yourself an "ihug" button and join the movement.

To purchase your "ihug" buttons and join the movement visit **www.ihugBook.com**

Epilogue

"Communication is at the core of every personal moment,
experience, transaction and interaction."
~Bob Nicoll

I have known LuAnn since the 2007 BNI International Conference in San Diego. She is as advertised – a dynamic package of energy, passion, and warmth—and one of the quickest to welcome a stranger with an embrace. In the 3600 plus days we have known each other, I have watched her hugging energy shift the paradigm in the room.

The first time I met her at conference, she gave me a great hug, and I instantly knew I had a cherished friend. A hug is the universal language of support, care, great to see you, and for the first timers; great to meet you.

In Chapter 4, LuAnn describes 'the best hug ever'. I am humbled she included comments about Remember the Ice and the power of removing the "k-not-y" words from our speaking and writing. It is a powerful concept and I appreciate her including it.

In Remember the Ice and Other Paradigm Shifts, Chapter 9 is the last chapter and is titled:

THE NEXT RIGHT THING,
How to Use the Tools You Now Have

So now you have acquired all these empowering tools for changing your life. What are you going to do with them? You can shift your paradigms now, so it's time to figure out what to shift them to.

In this final chapter you will learn about the importance of doing the next right thing. That is, shifting your paradigms so that you are an even more productive, contributing, participating member of society. You have the ability within you to make a difference. You can create anything you want for yourself, and now I would like you to consider the power in creating good for the world around you.

A simple paradigm shift can change your reality, allowing your mind to entertain new ideas and recognize possibilities that were previously hidden because they had no way in before you opened your mind.

Doing the next right thing is simply continuing the process and the pattern of empowering yourself and those around you.

Changing your own future is just the beginning. I believe that with great empowerment comes great responsibility and great respond-ability. Empowered word choice will give you what you want. Choose your words carefully.

Reflecting on these words from Chapter 9, I would add, 'choose your actions carefully' as well.

When Edward Lorenz proposed, in 1963, a theory of a butterfly flapping its wings on one side of the ocean could impact the weather on the other side, most people were skeptical at best. In the 1990's his work began to receive some authentication. The concept of "the Butterfly Effect" has now been granted the status of a law: The Law of Sensitive Dependence upon Initial Conditions.

When you feel a great connection with your spouse, children, co-workers, friends, in-laws, out-laws, whoever you decide – even over the phone or when thinking about them far away, you can send them a virtual hug in your mind and heart. What an amazing experience.

LuAnn created a connection with me with her initial condition of a hug. Over time we have become close friends and co-authors. We have collaborated on networking events, shared a passion for watching our favorite NFL teams – her Vikings and my Patriots – appreciated the April ritual of the Masters, and worked with numerous colleagues mentioned on sharing the power of getting connected.

Now we aspire to be a part of the Hug Movement on a global scale. Think of the impact you'll have when you demonstrate your respond-ability by giving your strength and love and compassion through the simple, universal, caring act of a HUG.

Watch for more information to come on
www.globalhugday.com on this paradigm shifting
movement.

**Hug to Go…"Hugging is such a simple thing to do.
We need to hug it forward."~Bob Nicoll**

About the Author
The Little SPARK

LuAnn Buechler, CMP, Author, Master Trainer, Coach and Transformational Speaker

"Sparking break-through change in you and your organization!"

Passionate about everything she does. LuAnn uses her unique personality and experiences to relate to her audiences in delivering passionate presentations that inspire people to achieve the success they desire in business and in life, by helping them Live their personal SPARK!

As a Certified Facilitator of The Passion Test, LuAnn shares with audiences a simply yet powerful system to determine your true passions and set a course to living your life's destiny.

As a Certified Facilitator of the Passion Test for Business, LuAnn is Igniting the Heart of Business. Bringing to life the unique contribution of the businesses she works with while aligning their team to their personal passions to create a company culture that thrives in today's business environment.

As a Director Consultant for BNI, LuAnn has built a repertoire of presentations on networking skills and relationship marketing which she uniquely relates to delivering high quality customer service.

LuAnn delivers Customer Service training with the same passion that she delivers customer service in her own event management business. LuAnn has over 25 years of experience in the Hospitality Industry, and is the Co-Author of ***Exceptional Care for Your Valued Clients***.

LuAnn is also a member of the Transformational Leadership Council working team. An organization created by Jack Canfield, best-selling author of the Chicken Soup for the Soul series, where transformational leaders share best practices and co-create humanitarian projects to transform the world.

www.LuAnnB.com

LuAnn@LuAnnB.com

Edifications

Janet Bray Attwood, Co-author with Chris Attwood of the NY Times bestseller, *The Passion Test: The Effortless Path to Discovering Your Life Purpose*. CEO of Enlightened Alliances, the parent company for all Passion Test Programs and Founding Member of the TLC.

Barnet Bain, Director, Milton's Secret, Author, The Book of Doing and Being: Rediscovering Creativity in Life, Love and Work. TLC Member.

Patty Blakesley, Author, Poet, Passion Test and Passion Test for Business Facilitator, Co-creator of the Inspired Women's Writing Retreats with LuAnn.

Jack Canfield, American author, motivational speaker, seminar leader, corporate trainer, and entrepreneur. He is a multiple New York Times bestselling author, and founder Chicken Soup for the Soul® Enterprises & The Canfield Training Group. Founding Member of the TLC

Gary D. Chapman, *New York Times* bestselling Author of *The Five Love Languages* series.

Lori Colwill, owner of Digidoodle Designs, website and graphics design business. Lori manages LuAnn's design needs and website and is a dear friend.

Rick Foster is President of Foster, Hicks & Associates, a leadership, team, and organizational consultancy. He works in global corporations and medical centers worldwide where he helps create high trust, high performance teams and networks.

Kevin Frieberg, Best Selling Author, Thought Leader and Professional Speaker. In his international best seller, *NUTS! Southwest Airlines' Crazy Recipe for Business and Personal Success*, Dr. Freiberg uncovered the strategies that created the greatest success story in the history of commercial aviation.

Lisa Garr has dedicated her life to the awareness of herself and her surroundings. In 1999, she created The Aware Show, a talk radio show about natural health, personal growth and spirituality on KPFK 90.7fm. She is also the author of *Becoming Aware*.

Brian Hillard, loving husband to Arielle Ford (TLC Member) who enjoys living in La Jolla, CA and is a passionate advocate for the disenfranchised.

Hana Honda, daughter of **Ken Honda**, the author of more than 60 best-selling self-development books on lifework, life balance, wealth, and happiness.

Mabel Iam, renowned Author of *The Love Diet*®. Mabel Iam is a psychotherapist, a romance therapist, adviser and expert in relationships, as well as a successful hostess and producer for TV and radio shows. Four-time winning Latin Literary Award and social media marketing strategy expert.

Kathleen Keating, Author of *The Hug Therapy* book series, and many other intriguing self-help books and novels.

Carol Kline, contributing author of the *NY Times* bestseller *Love for No Reason*, by Marci Shimoff.

Karin Lubin is now the General Manager for Enlightened Alliances, the organization under which all Passion Test programs are run and supporting Janet Bray Attwood

Robert MacPhee is a speaker, author, coach, and consultant. He is the creator of the Excellent Decisions leadership development program that teaches people how to make decisions based on their vision and values rather than all of the stress and pressure they are faced with. He is a Founding Member and former Executive Director of the Transformational Leadership Council and a co-founder of the Southern California Association of Transformational Leaders. Robert's *Manifesting for Non-Gurus* book and partner journal have helped thousands of people to more quickly and easily create more of the results they most want in their lives.

Dr. Ivan Misner is the Founder and Chief Visionary Officer of BNI. BNI was founded in 1985. The organization has over thousands of chapters throughout the world. Each year, BNI generates over millions of referrals resulting in over billions of dollars worth of business for its members. He has written 21 books, including his *New York Times* best seller, *Truth or Delusion* and his #1 bestseller, *Masters of Success*. Founding Member of the TLC.

Dr. Sue Morter, Founder and President of the Morter Institute, International speaker, Master of Bio-Energetic Medicine and Quantum Field visionary, Dr. Sue utilizes the embodiment of high frequency energy patterns to activate full human potential.

Z. Newell, Author & Inspirational Speaker, PassionPoweredLife.com, WhatMadeMeThink.com, Author of BRINK: Don't Go Back to Sleep and soon to be released: The MQformula: How to Ignite Your Magnificence Quotient!

Bob Nicoll, is a Wordsmith, Author and Creator of Remember the Ice. He has authored *Remember the Ice and Other Paradigm Shifts* and co-authored *Exceptional Care for Your Valued Client* with LuAnn.

Marc Pletzer, Communication trainer, NLP master trainer and enthusiasm coach, managing director of Fresh-academy GmbH. Bestselling Author and TLC Member.

don Miguel Ruiz, Author of the *Four Agreements,* is also the author of *The Mastery of Love, The Voice of Knowledge, Prayers,* and the *New York Times* bestseller, *The Fifth Agreement,* a collaboration with his son, don José Ruiz.

Martin Rutte, Founder of the HeavenonEarth.com Project. Martin is a dynamic, international speaker and consultant on spirituality in the workplace. Member of the TLC.

Marci Shimoff, Author of the *NY Times* bestseller *Love for No Reason,* by Marci Shimoff with Carol Kline. Member of the TLC.

Guy Stickney is the founder and CEO of WizardryEvents, a company that has produced conferences all over the world over the past 13 years. TLC Meetings Director and Member.

Ruth Tongen, owner Synergy Health, Ruth has more than 25 years of health care experience. She is also a Passion Test & Passion Test for Business Facilitator and dear friend.

Doreen Virtue, is an American author and a motivational speaker. She is the founder of Angel Therapy. Virtue has written over 50 books including oracle cards, oracle decks on the subject of angels and other spiritual topics.

GP Walsh is a Speaker, Author, Leader, Spiritual Teacher, Meditation Master, EFT Expert and Composer. GP Walsh is a master storyteller and a TLC Member.

Tony Wolfe, Man of a thousand voices...give or take a few. Tony Wolfe is a voice over artist based in the Orlando, Florida, area and heard all around the globe, including several Fortune 500 companies.

Made in the USA
Middletown, DE
06 February 2020

84268661R00044